Once upon a time there was a handsome kitten born in Sacramento, California. He was a special cat because he was a Bengal.

A Bengal is a type of cat breed that is very exotic. It is a cross between a house cat, and an Asian Leopard Cat.

D1486826

Sonny had a lot of spots and some stripes too.
Just like all of his brothers and sisters.

Sonny sure loved to eat. He would always come running when he heard a can of food being opened.

He loved to eat as fast as he could, sometimes a little too fast.

But eventually, Sonny learned he could take his time eating, so he could properly digest his food.

Once Sonny got big enough, he was ready to go out in the world and find a good family to be part of. Sonny and his brother Luca, who he loved very much, were picked to live together with a wonderful family in San Rafael, California.

One stormy day, a boy named Elliott came to pick them up in his Jeep. They all drove off together to their new home.

When they got there, they were welcomed by the rest of the family. A girl named Erica, a gentleman named Roman, and a lady named Beverly. Sonny and Luca found their new home to be spacious, clean and fun.

Their new family were all so nice, and they always had good food.

Sonny and Luca started to get to know their new surroundings by walking around their new room, the rest of the house, and then eventually learned what being outside was like.

Learning to hunt and play was so much fun. The Bengal boys loved to run, jump, climb and chase each other around the house and outside.

They even took to fishing rubber ducks from the family swimming pool!

Their new life sure was great.

Until one morning. Sonny and Luca went on a long walk, but something was not right.

They realized they were not alone on the path.

In a matter of seconds, a predator chased after Luca. Luca quickly told Sonny to run with all of his might back home to get their family to help. Sonny was scared, but he ran home as fast as he could.

But it was too late. Sonny and his family spent the next two days looking for poor Luca. They never found him.

The loss of Luca made them all so sad. Sonny missed his brother, and wished he could have done something to save him. Sonny had a broken heart, so the family took him to the doctor.

When Sonny returned home there was an unfamiliar scent in the house. *What could it be?* Sonny thought. And then he saw another kitten like himself! Except it was a girl, with a beautiful silver-gray coat.

Sonny was excited to have a friend to play and snuggle with again. His new friend's name was Connie, she was so sweet, petite, and lovely.

Connie cheered them up so much that they were able to move on and be happy again. While the loss of Luca would always be with Sonny and his family, they became stronger and agreed to be more aware of their surroundings.

Now Sonny and Connie happily play together all the time.

They even take comfortable and safe harnessed walks around the neighborhood and they always say hello to friendly dogs and neighbors they see. They eat together, hunt together, nap together, and have many, many snuggles with their loving family.

The End

Dedicated to Luca.
Forever missed and in our hearts.

Written by Erica Starno
Edited by Elliott Starno
Illustrated by Stevie Mahardhika
Layout by Elliott Starno
December 2017

© 2019 by Erica Starno. All rights reserved.

Draw Sonny on this page!

Draw Connie on this page!

CPSIA information can be obtained
at www.ICGtesting.com
Printed in the USA
BVHW060140231019
561814BV00003BA/7/P